Lessons From Life:
A Teacher's Story

Roger DiBattista, B.A. B.ED.

Lessons From Life - A Teacher's Story
Copyright © 2021 by Roger DiBattista, B.A. B.ED.

All rights reserved. No part of this publication may be
reproduced, distributed, or transmitted in any form or
by any means, including photocopying, recording, or
other electronic or mechanical methods, without the prior
written permission of the author, except in the case of
brief quotations embodied in critical reviews and certain
other non-commercial uses permitted by copyright law.

Tellwell Talent
www.tellwell.ca

ISBN
978-0-2288-4955-1 (Hardcover)
978-0-2288-4957-5 (Paperback)
978-0-2288-4956-8 (eBook)

Table of Contents

Acknowledgements

I would like to take this opportunity to thank everyone who has helped me along the way, my parents, Emidio and Antonietta DiBattista first and foremost, for their love and support, my sister and brother-in-law Lea and Albert for all their guidance and understanding, my wife Eveline who has always been my 'rock' and who has helped me unconditionally, my daughter and son-in-law Alicia and Peter, who have always inspired me and encouraged me to be the best that I can be and all of my friends who have been there for me through the years. I would also like to thank Jody Aberdeen for his assistance in this project.

My Family...My Loves!

Introduction

I've lived a great life, and I feel very lucky to be here. That's why I want to share my story with you.

There's a lyric from an old song that speaks to me:

'We're only here for a good time, not a long time. So have a good time because the sun doesn't shine everyday." (Trooper, 1979)

That has never been truer than when you're born with a life-threatening medical condition. You treasure every day that you're alive.

I was born with hydrocephalus. According to the National Institute Of Neurological Disorders and Stroke, hydrocephalus is defined as, 'a condition in which the primary characteristic is excessive accumulation of cerebrospinal fluid (CSF) -- the clear fluid that surrounds the brain and spinal cord. This excessive accumulation results in an abnormal dilation of the spaces in the brain called ventricles. This dilation causes potentially harmful pressure on the tissues of the brain.' As a result, I began experiencing a variety of different health problems, including severe headaches, vision problems, vomiting, seizures, and damage to mental functioning, to name just a few.

At the time that I was born, treatments for hydrocephalus were still experimental, and even then, doctors would often tell parents that their babies only had a few months or a year to live.

And yet, I'm still here.

In this book, you'll read seven short stories from different parts of my life with hydrocephalus.

I wrote this book for all of the young people out there who are going through something like this, not only those with hydrocephalus, but who have cancer, autoimmune diseases, and other physical or developmental disabilities.

I want to share my story of lost summers and long stays at the hospital to show that you're not alone in what you're going through. I also want to show you what's possible for you in your future: finding a passion for your life, meeting the partner of your dreams, and all the amazing experiences that you might think aren't possible for you where you are now.

My message to anyone suffering any kind of an illness or setback is 'never give up, work to your capacity and do what you can to fulfill your life dreams. After all, we only get to do this once.'

New Life In Canada

I was born in Hamilton, Ontario, Canada on July 30, 1953, the second child and first son of immigrant parents.

My parents, Emidio and Antonietta DiBattista, were originally from a little town called Castiglione a Casauria, in the region of Abruzzo, in their beloved homeland of Italy.

My parents married and shortly after, World War II broke out. My father enlisted in the army and was gone until the war was over in 1945. After returning home safely, two years later, my sister Lea was born in Italy.

After the end of the war, many of my relatives had started leaving Italy for a fresh start overseas, a choice that my parents started to contemplate for themselves. We had more than a few family members choose to come to Canada (and Hamilton in particular) as well as the United States, where my mother's brother and her own mother emigrated in order to start over and raise their families.

My parents kept in touch with them and in those conversations, almost every single one of them said that there was a better life in Canada. A few of my cousins who had already been in Canada confirmed with us that life was much better, with more opportunities for their children.

Even though my mom was expecting, my parents made the decision to make the journey to Canada and start a new life in this wonderful country that had taken such good care of our other family members who'd come before. They made all the arrangements and said their goodbyes to their ancestral home, and boarded a ship called the *Saturnia* just a few months before I was born.

The *Saturnia* docked in Halifax in May, 1953. My uncle, my mom's brother and his family had been living in Hamilton for some time, and so my parents decided it made the most sense to head inland. Upon arriving, they were welcomed and lived with my aunt and uncle, with whom they stayed until they could settle themselves and until I was born in July. It was because of that choice that I was born in this city that I still call home to this day. Not long after that, we moved to Gertrude Street in Hamilton where we rented for a time.

Then, as now, immigrants faced many hardships. My parents were now in a foreign country, spoke no English, and did not have employment right away. They say that no one understands hard work like an immigrant, and this was very true for my parents, who set out to make a life for themselves and for my sister and I as best they could.

My father, as strong and determined as he was, immediately found work in construction with a firm that he stayed with for a long time. Later on, he would work at the Hamilton Forum arena as an ice maker, and later as a foreman. The time came when my parents were able to buy a house on Clinton Street, where we lived for a very long time. Within only a few months of arriving in Canada, my family seemed to adjust to their new life here as immigrants as best they could.

Three months after I was born, however, is when things started to unravel.

I was a baby, so I have no direct recollection of this, but when I was three months old, my mother noticed that my skull was starting to enlarge, and not in a normal way. My parents took me to the doctor right away.

After a very quick examination, he looked at them. "This baby needs to be hospitalized immediately," he said.

My parents hadn't learned English yet, and so they set out to find an Italian- speaking pediatrician. We were connected to a Dr. F.A Olivieri, who at the time was practising on Barton Street near Kinrade in the east end of Hamilton.

As soon as Dr. Olivieri looked at my skull, he knew how serious this was. "You need to take him to the Hospital for Sick Children in Toronto," he said to them in Italian. "There is a specialist there who can help with this condition. It's more complicated than what I can help you with here."

Following his referral, my parents took their first trip to Toronto that September and met with the specialist for an immediate consultation and treatment. It was there that I was first diagnosed with hydrocephalus.

"Unfortunately," said the specialist, "there's no cure for hydrocephalus. Left untreated, your baby will die in six months' time." They also told my parents that if I survived, I would have physical or mental limitations.

My parents were devastated, but God must have been on my side because of what the doctor said next. "However, there's a procedure we can try that might save his life."

The doctors, Dr. William Keith and Dr.

E. Bruce Hendrick, had told my parents at the time that Health Canada had been researching a procedure using a shunt to drain the fluid from the brain in cases like this. My parents were skeptical, but were convinced this was the only way to save my life. Therefore, with their permission, they proceeded to diagnose, operate, and insert said shunt to drain the fluid.

My parents were informed that this was one of the first, if not *the* first shunt operation, and that it was purely experimental. The procedure itself took approximately 90 minutes. Thankfully, the doctors told my parents that the surgery was successful and that I was recovering well.

My parents were informed of the risks and what would follow, but it was extremely hard on them both. Not only would they have to cope with being new to Canada, learn the language, and confront every other challenge faced by newcomers, but they would now also be forced to navigate an unfamiliar health care system and find a way to meet my complex needs.

Trips to the Hospital for Sick Children from Hamilton were not an easy task for my family since no one drove. We needed to enlist the help of my cousins who had been in the country for a few years. They knew their way to Toronto and therefore volunteered to drive us there. With the help of family members who acted as interpreters on their behalf, the doctors would explain all the procedures that would take place as well as keeping them updated as to how effective the treatments were being. Whenever I would get new symptoms or challenges, my Canadian relatives were there for us to make sure everyone could communicate clearly.

Though the shunt saved my life and prevented my skull from swelling further, it came with a lot of side effects. In those early years, I remember having many severe migraine headaches, and I was vomiting a lot, almost every day. Hydrocephalus also made me very sensitive to sounds. It was so bad that when people would come over to visit and I couldn't stand the noise, I would run up to my room to find some relief.

Every so often, the shunt would get blocked and fluid would start building up again, so I would have to go back to The Hospital for Sick Children for a lumbar puncture, where they would put a needle in between two of my vertebrae to remove excess fluid. It was extremely painful, especially for a child. Whenever they did that, I saw stars. It was awful. I had to get three or four of those in my lifetime, and those procedures are one of the reasons why my back is so weak today.

There was one time in particular when I was seven years of age that my parents were in the room when I got the lumbar puncture. I was screaming so loudly that my Dad couldn't stay in the room and watch me suffer. My father was a very strong but sensitive man and he hated to see me in that condition. My mother was a pillar of strength. She was right there the whole time. She would hold my hand and she would tell me, in Italian, "Don't worry, it'll be all right".

This became the rhythm that my early years would follow.

My earliest memories were when I was six years old. I was in school. There was no such thing as junior or senior kindergarten at the time, so every child started elementary school in Grade 1.

That first year at school was a blur, because for much of it, I was in and out of the hospital all the time so I missed many classes. In fact, I still have old report cards from each term that say "missed 35 days", "missed 45 days", etc... I even had one that read, "Promoted to Grade 2, but on trial". I had three months to prove that I had learned enough in Grade 1 with all the time I had missed to stay in Grade 2, otherwise they would keep me back a year to make up for the lost classroom time. Even back then I was bound and determined not to be left behind a year.

Sensory sensitivity, especially to noise, was also one of the reasons why I couldn't sit in the classroom for too long. Anytime the teacher would speak too loudly, or if the kids were talking and making noise in between lessons, it would be overwhelming for me. There were no "special needs" options in elementary school back then, so I had to stay in the regular class with everyone else.

No one could have known it at the time (I certainly couldn't) that I would more than make up all those lost days in the classroom years later, when I would become a teacher.

Put your trust in your family. They will treat you the right way. I found comfort in my family. If it wasn't for them, I don't think I would have survived.

Even if you don't have your parents or cousins around, "family" can be anyone who is in your life – friends and caregivers – who are there for you when you need them. I am especially grateful for my sister Lea, who growing up always had my back no matter what, and still does to this day.

Things are better now. I believe the system has gotten much better since then. Back in the day, some nurses and doctors had terrible bedside manners. If you were a child who was ill and complained of pain, they treated you like you were in school, telling you to be quiet and that everything would be fine. They'd come in with the needles for painkillers. When it was afternoon naptime, you were told to close your eyes and try to sleep. I tried several times to listen to my little transistor radio with my earphones, but the nurse would come in and scold me and tell me to 'turn that off and go to sleep.' That's the way it was.

Our system, of course, is not perfect.

There are always ways to improve it. Sometimes, it may let you down. However, compared to where it was before, we are very lucky to have the healthcare system of 2020.

For example, my parents had to go back and forth to Toronto and I was left alone quite often. Before, it was taboo: you did not stay with your child. When visiting hours were over, my parents were asked to leave. I hated the thought of not seeing my parents until the next day. That's just the way it was. If you wanted to, you'd come back the next day.

Today, we have places like Ronald McDonald House in Hamilton that allow parents who have come in from far away for their child's treatment to stay overnight. I know people who have children with severe problems and they get to spend the night with them.

It's also easier for newcomers. Today there are all sorts of assistance given to newcomers to help them climatize themselves to this new country. In my parents' case, neither one of them drove until later. In fact, my mom got a licence at the age of 55 just to help me out with insurance so I could be a secondary driver with her car. The resources to help them get that kind of training and development that we have today just weren't around back them.

As hard as it may be to believe sometimes, there really hasn't ever been a better time to be alive than today. We've come a long way since 1953, and so it's important to look at what's working and to find gratitude wherever you can.

Shindigs and Lost Summers

Between the ages of 6 and 17, I spent nearly every single one of my summer holidays in hospital. If it wasn't one thing, it was something else.

Near the end of the school year, the kids in my classes would start talking about their plans for summer vacation. Many would be heading up north to the cottage or on road trips to the States and other parts of Canada. Others would be going to camp or beaches and other places. I was happy for them, but it was hard for me sometimes to hear about all the things I was missing out on.

Often, around that same time of year, I'd have another new symptom pop up that would require me going to the doctor, who would then send me to the hospital for treatment.

What makes hydrocephalus such a terrible condition is that it causes all sorts of different health problems. I knew, usually before the end of the school year, that I would definitely be spending a couple of weeks in hospital in July and then a follow up in August, meaning my whole summer was ruined.

Between the ages of 6 and 9, most of my problems were neurological. The shunt, though it worked, caused migraine headaches, and so I would have lumbar punctures every summer.

The doctors also noted though "he's going to have physical difficulties, too."

When I was 9 years old, my left eye started to become crossed. I remember one day, I was out playing with kids when one of them frowned.

'Are you making faces at me?' he asked.

"No," I said. "Why?"

"Well, your one eye is looking at me, but your other one going the other way."

I hadn't really noticed anything weird, but I went to show my Mom and she took a look at me. We went to see Dr.

Olivieri, who took a close look at the eye. "This is a result of the hydrocephalus," he said. "You'll need to take him back to Toronto."

I went back to the Hospital for Sick Children and had to get an ophthalmologist to look at it. The conclusion was grim. "We have to do surgery," he said.

The procedure itself, I don't remember, but I never forgot that I had two patches over both eyes for three weeks. It was awful. I didn't know if it was day or night. I would often call out to the nurse, asking about the time. "Is it 3 o'clock in the morning or in the afternoon?" I really didn't know.

My parents were always there for me and this particular time I was a huge fan of the Beatles and so I had asked them if I could have the newest Beatles album, 'Beatles VI'. My parents always tried to make me happy. They knew how upset I was for being in the hospital yet again, so I was surprised when they came with the album to the hospital. I remember that I had written down the name of the album on a piece of paper, so I guess my sister had bought it for them to give to me. I still had the patches on my eyes but I knew what was waiting for me when they came off! I couldn't wait to get home to listen to it on my portable record player. After the doctors took the patches off, I was fine, except that I had to wear glasses, permanently. That was one summer.

One other example that stands out in my mind was when I was 11 years old, just two years after the eye surgery. I was on my way to school toward the end of the school year when all of a sudden, my left foot just flipped over. Imagine you're walking normally one minute, and then the next, your foot just decides to turn around so that you're putting your weight on one side.

That's what happened to me, out of nowhere. I lost control of it. I started walking on the side of my foot.

My friends told me that I must have had a "club foot", but I didn't know what that meant. Once again, my parents, as diligent as they were, took me back to Sick Kids, where the doctor said my condition was actually known as "drop foot". As with my eyes, the doctors would need to perform surgery to correct it. They had to fuse my ankle in order to make my foot stand flat on the ground again.

Again, I don't remember much about the surgery itself, but once again, I was inside and off my feet during the rest of that summer while I recovered. To this day, whereas most people can flex their feet back and forth, I am unable to do that on that foot.

After each stay in hospital, I would come home and then not really go anywhere. My backyard and my street became my universe. That was my summertime, for nearly 17 years.

If you're a young person reading this who's lost a summer or two in the hospital, you know how hard it is. Even though today, we have a lot more activities and devices like iPads, video games, books, and television to keep busy, it's still very difficult to stay cooped up in a hospital bed or at home with nowhere else to go besides your backyard, knowing that other children are out there enjoying the sunshine and playing outdoors.

It's natural and okay to feel sad, and it's also important to develop a coping strategy during such times to help get you through.

Coping mechanisms are important.

While I was in hospital, I didn't have anything except my little transistor radio. I would listen to it to help me pass the time. In fact, I remember being scolded by the nurses for listening to my radio with my earphones on during nap time. They were like wardens, who would bellow,'turn that off. It's time to rest!' You didn't dare defy them. Nowadays, as I said, there are a lot more ways to keep you busy, but if you don't have those things, the important thing is to make long lasting friendships while you're in the hospital.

It's important that you have that group of people who will help you not feel alone while you're in the hospital. Get out there and make friends, even if they're in the next room. I'm outgoing, so it's easy for me, but for the child who isn't, it may be more difficult, but you have to force yourself.

Once you're in that situation, you have no choice but to get out there and basically say, "Here I am. Why don't we do something together?"

If you're in long term hospital care, that's what I'd suggest. When you get out of the hospital, find new things that you can do for yourself. I had many friends who were playing football and baseball. I couldn't do any of those things.

I also developed some coping mechanisms while at home. The time you spend recovering from a health operation can mean that you can't go on family trips to the beach or to

Niagara Falls or other places. Your home becomes a new place that you can't leave.

My parents bought me a portable record player, and we used to put it in the backyard. I would play music and then get the neighbourhood kids over. That was my way of compensating for not being able to do anything else. The only ones who really understood me were my friends from the neighbourhood.

I would have "shindigs" in my backyard, named after a TV show that was popular in the 60's. It was one of those dance party shows where they would play the latest music and show people dancing to it. I'd set up the record player and kids from the neighbourhood would come by and dance up a storm.

If it was sunny out, we'd have our shindig in the backyard, and whenever it rained, my parents were good enough to let us take the party into the house. They never said anything. My parents always did everything they could to make me happy.

Even though my sister Lea, is six years older than I am, I remember one time that she and her girlfriend Norma Jean were kind enough to come and help out to make sure that we were having a good time and that everything was running smoothly. Some of my friends included Wayne from two doors down, the first friend I made in the neighbourhood, and a cluster of friends from around the corner of the block.

Some of them included Jeff, who I used to call my 'guardian angel' because he was the strong one of the group and always looked out for me. On the neighbouring street, Barnesdale Avenue, I had close friends such as Philip, Anne-Marie, MaryAnne, and Joe. I was always welcome in their homes. They all understood my situation and were so accepting of it and made me feel like I was one of them.

There was also my cousin Rita on my dad's side of the family, who would come by all the time. Rita was like a second sister to me. She lived on the corner of Clinton and Barnesdale and about six houses away from me. She and her friend MaryAnne would always come running up to my parents whenever they got home, asking "When's Roger coming home from the hospital? When's Roger coming home from the hospital?"

Rita was very helpful to me when I was on crutches from my foot surgery. When school started in September she would come by my house and we would walk to school together and she would carry my books for me since I couldn't manage. We were the same age and sometimes we were even in the same class.

My birthdays were also special. I was born in July, so for the years where I was at home and not in the hospital, we would always have a big party. Somehow, I managed to always be home from the hospital on my birthday. I remember that I never had a rainy day on my birthday, which made me feel lucky.

For my 11th birthday, the year I had my ankle surgery, Mom made an amazing chocolate cream cake from scratch. I can still taste how good it was! To this day I believe it is the best cake I've ever had. We'd have chips and popcorn, fruit punch and pop. My parents spared no expense. Whatever I wanted to have, they always did for me.

For this reason and to this day, birthdays are very important to me and therefore I always celebrate my birthday because I feel I'm celebrating another year that I am alive. Nowadays, my friend Paul will joke with me and say, 'So, Roger, are you going to celebrate your birthday for a whole year?'

One of my friends in particular that I mentioned earlier had a very creative streak in him. Wayne was a smart young man who always had these great ideas for things we could do. Even back then, I had a soft spot for Sick Kids Hospital, because they'd helped me so much.

One day, Wayne told me, "You know what we should do? Let's do a fundraiser for the hospital!"

"I like that idea!" I said. "What kind of fundraiser do you want to do?"

Wayne thought for a moment and then said, "Well, why don't we do a haunted house? We could charge people a quarter to come in and walk through it and then give that money to the hospital."

My parents loved the idea, and so we set it up. We created scary decorations with whatever we could find: paper, spaghetti, and even Jello. We would blindfold people and lead them through a scary "tour".

It was a lot of fun. We managed to raise $55 dollars, which my parents donated to Sick Kids Hospital on my behalf. I remember receiving a letter of thanks from the hospital for the donation.

When the haunted house worked, Wayne and I had another idea: we put on a murder mystery play in my backyard.

Wayne called it "Blood and Black Lace", for reasons I can't remember. I was the protagonist who tried to solve the case. We even held auditions for other parts in the play for the other kids in the neighbourhood. We really got into the spirit of things and put on two performances, in the afternoon and in the evening. That time, we managed to make $60 or $70 dollars each time, which also went to Sick Kids' Hospital. They were very appreciative and, I think, touched by our donations.

Giving back became another way to cope with those lost summers. If you are in a position to help someone else while you're going through your own challenges, it takes away a lot of the bad feelings and helps you pass the time. In that way, I never quite lost my childhood summers, but made the most of them the best way that I could.

Wayne and I lost touch with each other for a long time. He moved away from the neighbourhood in 1968 and I never saw him again. I was devastated that I had lost my closest friend, but through the magic of Facebook, just a few years ago, we managed to reconnect, and we're friends again.

Wayne lives in Toronto now, and has come to visit me every so often.

I had a very good nucleus of friends in my neighbourhood. If it hadn't had been for the people I grew up with, the friends I made in university later on - such as Tony, Paul, and Karl (who are still my best friends today and a group of girls with whom I became good friends, Joanna, Mena, Sara, Tina, and

Pam, also students in the Humanities program in university with me - my self esteem would have been zero.

That's why I always tell children who have a disability or a health condition to do whatever they can to make friends. Set aside your limitations as best you can, forge ahead, and make friends. You don't need to have a lot of friends either. My mom would always say that "you don't have to have ten friends. If you only have one or two good friends that you can rely on when you need them, you're rich".

When you go through enough hard times, you can develop a thick skin that causes you to harden your heart. As important as family is, the thing about friends is that you can get to choose them, and if you can practise putting yourself out there and meeting new people, whether it's the kid in the hospital bed next to you or the kids two houses down, you'll have people who will keep you happy and open-hearted.

I met such a friend when I was in the hospital for my ankle surgery. His name was Randy, someone who's gone now, but whom I'll never forget.

Randy

Every child has a coming of age moment, a time or incident or event in their young lives when they're forever changed afterwards, something or someone that they never forget.

For a young boy who was in and out of the hospital, a child who didn't have an ordinary childhood, my coming of age happened when I met Randy.

It was the summer that I turned 11 and I was back in Toronto, at the Hospital for Sick Children, for yet another treatment to deal with a condition stemming from hydrocephalus. Every summer, as I've said, was something different. This time, it was to have surgery for "drop foot", a condition where, out of nowhere, my left foot begam to twist in a way that prevented me from walking properly.

It was a hot July day when I was admitted to the hospital. Once again, while my school friends and cousins got to play and travel and enjoy the warm summer days, I was stuck inside, in pain and discomfort, missing out on nearly everything.

Settled into my bed, my parents had gone home, and I was just sitting there, wallowing in self-pity. The curtain around my bed was drawn and I could see the bed across from me. There was another boy sitting there, reading a comic, and otherwise just minding his own business.

Feeling sad and alone, I started to cry. I tried to keep quiet, but I must have gotten a little loud because after not too long, I heard a voice say "What are you crying for?"

I looked up and saw the other boy staring at me. He had short brown hair, like me, and seemed really concerned about me by the expression on his face.

"I don't want to be here," I said in between sobs."

The boy nodded. "Join the club." "Well," I said, trying to get control of myself, wiping my tears away, "I don't want to be here. I'm missing my family and friends."

"You're not from Toronto?" the boy asked.

I shook my head. "No, I'm from Hamilton," choking back tears.

"Oh, okay," said the boy. "I'm not from around here either."

"Where are you from?" I asked. "Whitby." He paused for a second.

"What are you in for?"

"I have hydrocephalus," I replied.

The boy kind of cocked his head sideways. "Oh yeah?"

"Yeah."

"Me too." He smiled.

That was the moment I remember that he and I connected. We were both from out of town, here in this room together, far away from our families. And, we were both here for the same condition.

I stopped crying completely now, and the boy got up out of bed and stood up slowly. He was a tall kid, maybe 5'8", definitely a little taller than I was.

"Do you like to read?" he asked. "Yeah," I said.

"What kinds of books?"

My sister had bought me the whole series of Hardy Boys books, and I brought three of them to the hospital. I reached over to the bedside table where I had them within reach and picked up the one on the top of the pile.

"I like to read anything," I said." "In these ones, two kids, brothers, go around solving mysteries."

The boy held up the comic book he was reading.

"I'll trade you," he said. "Sure," I replied.

He came over to the bed and handed me his comic, and I gave him the one Hardy Boys book. He went back to his bed.

"My name's Roger," I said to him. "I'm Randy," he said, and then got under his blanket and started to read.

I smiled and then started reading the comic book he'd given me (I forget what it was.

It was the start of a friendship I'll never forget, even if it was short.

Randy's hydrocephalus hadn't acted up in the way that mine had. He didn't have drop foot or any other complications happen to him the way they had for me, at least not that I knew about. Still, we were kids and we didn't really spend a lot of time talking about the disease, at least not from what I remember. What mattered more was that we kept each other company. Not only that, we also had a lot of fun!

I remember we started doing very silly things in the hospital.

One morning, only a few days into my stay, Randy came up to me with wide eyes and a big grin. "Do you want to race wheelchairs down the hallway?"

With no hesitation, I said "yup!".

We would get in our wheelchairs and head to one end of the corridor.

"Ready! Set! Go!" one of us would say, and we were off, doing our best to outmaneuver and get ahead of each other, almost running into people and objects as we did.

The nurses, as you can imagine, weren't happy with us. In fact, they would get really angry each time!

"You boys stop that, right now!" they would bellow from the top of their lungs. Then they would grab the handles of our wheelchairs before we could get to the finish line, and push us back into our rooms.

Randy and I didn't care how much trouble we got into, though. We were laughing the whole time.

Our friendship blossomed from there.

I would see him every day and we would hang out. In fact, being just one bed over, we saw each other all the time. I remember we would talk about nearly everything – comic books heroes, sports, school, all sorts of stuff even though I can't remember exactly everything now looking back all these years later.

I went into the hospital in early July and stayed until the end of the month. It's funny: you can get to know someone in a month and you can get close to them quickly. Even to this day, I become friends very quickly with people. Maybe it's because of my upbringing or because I always cherish friendships. That's just the way I am. Either way, my friendship with Randy, though only lasting a few weeks, seemed like a lifetime, as if I'd gotten back all of that time that I'd lost that I could have spent playing and laughing with my friends.

By the end of July, I'd had my surgery.

I don't actually remember there being much of a dramatic moment when the time came to say goodbye to him. I imagine it would be something like his sitting in bed, reading one of his comics, while I gathered my things and waved goodbye to him, both of us smiling.

Back then, we were just kids. There was no "Hey, give me your number". Cellphones hadn't been invented yet, and unless you lived down the street from each other, you didn't give out your home telephone number. We just didn't do that.

As I got into the car with my family and we drove back home to Hamilton, I wondered if Randy and I would ever see each other again.

If the surgery had gone as planned, I wouldn't have gone back a second time that summer, but as it turned out, my foot developed an infection within a few weeks of my being released, so I had to return in August to have that treated.

When I got back, I was put in a different room down the hall from Randy, who I didn't really see much during this second visit. The hospital was very strict. You were not allowed to visit someone else in another room in the hospital, even if they were down the hall. There weren't any trading books to read this time, no wheelchair races down the corridor. I couldn't keep in touch with him unless we happened to pass each other in the hallway, exchanging only little waves and maybe a "hello" here and there.

The treatment didn't last as long as the surgery, and they put me on antibiotics.

Lying in bed this time, I decided to make sure I would say a proper goodbye to Randy when it was time to leave.

That day arrived, with the antibiotics now wearing off, and my parents arriving soon to take me home, I walked down the hallway to Randy's room. I wanted to ask him about everything he had been up to, how he was feeling, what comics he'd read, anything I could think of just so I could talk and hang out with him awhile before leaving.

When I got to the door, one of the nurses stopped me. She said, "Oh, you can't go in there."

"Oh, it's okay," I said. "I won't cause any trouble. I'm leaving soon and I just want to say goodbye to my friend Randy."

The nurse simply looked at me. "I'm sorry, but Randy passed away."

The news cut me like a knife through my heart. I just stood their frozen.

I think I might have taken a step back, just in total shock, and the nurse just walked away.

As young as I was, I remember thinking that the nurse was just awful for just telling me without any sense of caring. There hadn't been any compassion in her voice.

She'd told me that my friend had died as if I had asked her what the weather was like.

This is how they talk to kids?

If something like this would have happened today, the children would certainly be going through therapy and all sorts of programs to help them understand why their friend passed away. That's what I believe kids need today. They need some counselling after something like this. You can't just tell a child "your friend passed away" without any explanation or caring.

Mom and Dad came to get me, and I just burst into tears. They led me to the car, where my sister was waiting for us.

"What are you crying for?" she asked me.

I said, "do you remember that boy Randy I hung out with?" "Yeah?"

"Well, I just found out he died." "Are you kidding?"

"No."

My family was so understanding. My mother tried to comfort me. She even offered to get hold of Randy's parents and send him something. I knew his last name at the time (I've forgotten it now, but back then, we didn't know how to reach them or where they lived. The hospital, certainly, wouldn't give out that information.

We got back to Hamilton to resume the rest of what was left of that summer. Even though I tried to enjoy the time that I had, Randy was never far from my mind.

If you're a young person reading this and you've lost a friend, I'm so very sorry.

Don't think of them as gone, but think of them as now being at peace. There's no more suffering, there's no more pain. If you think of it that way, it may ease the pain of them being gone. It may be hard to understand, too, and I get that. We don't always know what to say when people we love die, even as grown-ups, but it's important to try.

I had made many friends during that period of time in my life, but I never forgot my time with Randy. I had never experienced the death of a close friend until then in my short life.

To this day, I think of Randy and wonder if he is at peace now and no longer in pain.

My First Job!

For most teenagers, the summer job is an experience that everyone gets to talk about later in life.

Whenever they would come by to visit me at the house or when we would reconnect at school in the fall, my friends would tell me stories about being out there and working part time jobs.

Even to this day, the friends I still have will remember and talk about how they worked at Wonder Bread, Stelco and Dofasco in the summer or delivering flyers and newspapers or even mowing lawns and watering gardens. They'll talk about the way the city was back then, their old bosses, the excitement of when they got paid, and all the things they spent their money on that you can't get anymore.

Being in the hospital with my hydrocephalus complications nearly every summer, I don't have any stories like that. While my other friends worked or played hockey or football on the street, I would sit on my porch and listen to my transistor radio.

My love for music developed during those years. While I never played an instrument, I could name any 'Top 40' song on the radio, and I could hum a few bars if I wanted to. In my head, I had entire albums' worth of musical knowledge.

Though I didn't know it at the time, all those summers spent by the transistor radio were preparing me for my very first job, working as a disc jockey alongside Ian MacLean (otherwise known as Angus McKie) at the Hamilton Forum.

My dad always wanted to make me feel like I was the same as all of my other friends, in spite of my disability, and therefore, he made things happen for me.

The Hamilton Forum was one of the city's great arenas, hosting the Jr. A Hamilton Red Wings. Years later it was torn down. Today, if you go to the Forum's old location at Barton and Sanford, you'll find nothing but housing. That was where my dad worked, and where he would take me on public skating nights sometimes.

Overlooking the rink was the office, in which there was the DJ's booth. I said to my dad, "I want to work up there someday". I pointed up towards the booth.

"Alright," said Dad, "let me make a call."

He spoke to the office and I was hired to help with the music for public skating. That was the highlight of my weekends during that time.

My dad introduced me to Ian, who sat me down next to the DJ equipment, consisting of a record player, all sorts of cool controls and gadgets like something out of an episode of *Star Trek*, and, of course, the big microphone. "Here," he said, motioning to a chair beside him, "sit next to me and just watch what I do."

I spent the rest of that first night and the next few Saturdays in that chair, watching Ian work and getting into it. In between shifts, I would even go out and buy small records that were called 45's back then and give it to him. "Do you want to play some of mine?" I would ask, and Ian would almost always say "Sure!".

One Saturday night, we were sitting in the DJ booth as usual when he put a record on and then turned to me. "Okay, Roger," he said to me, "it's your turn".

"What?" I said, surprised. Ian gestured towards the door.

"I'm going to leave and get a snack," he said, "and I'm going to let you do all the announcing and the music." He smiled, patted me on the back, and then walked out of the booth, leaving me in charge.

I was surprised and a little nervous, but you know what? It was great! I had the best time of my life that night spinning the tunes. My friends would often make fun of me, saying "give him a microphone, he doesn't shut up." Well, now I actually did have a microphone.

I put on another 45 and then spoke into the mic. "Now we're going to listen to the Rolling Stones 'I Can't Get No Satisfaction', so get your skates on and let's see everyone grooving out there!".

After all those weeks of shadowing Ian, I pulled it off!

Public skating used to be three hours long. Ian would announce for an hour and a half, and I would take over for the second hour and a half. The announcements you'd hear would be whatever came into my head, just totally riffing. It was so much fun!

I'd have to instruct skaters at certain times. "Okay, skaters, stop, turn around, and skate the other way", because that was one of the things that my dad, who made the ice, wanted me to do. He didn't want people skating in the same direction to help with the ice conditions. It was a maintenance announcement, but I would still make it fun. "Now we're gonna listen to the Beatles' 'Day Tripper' while we start going the other way!".

I had that arrangement with Ian for two years. I would get paid something like

$4/hour. It wasn't much even back then, but I wasn't doing it for the money. It was something that I really loved to do. I wish I had continued doing something like this later on, even part time while teaching but as it happened, things changed.

When I was 16 years old, though, Ian ended up quitting his job. I don't remember if he'd talked to me or Dad about it before I found out, but all I know is that I went to work one day and they replaced him with someone new. Though I'm sure he was very nice, I didn't feel comfortable with the new person who replaced him, so I stopped going. My career as a skating arena DJ was finished.

By then, I'd started thinking about bigger career goals, especially of becoming a teacher. Part of me wishes that I had stayed longer in the music and being a DJ, because it was a great time, but it wasn't meant to be.

Getting the job at the rink was a big deal, then. It was something I'd wanted to do and I loved doing it. Thanks to my dad, I got a chance to do what I wanted to do for at least a couple of years.

My parents started saying to me around that time "if you want something, you've got to earn it".

Earlier on when I was younger, they'd get me whatever I wanted, but as I got older, they instilled responsibility in me. What I got from this was that I got some extra money, and if I wanted to buy something frivolous, I wouldn't have to ask my parents for the cash. I could spend it on a bag of chips, for example, or go to a movie. It taught me a little bit of responsibility at that age. But if I ever needed anything important, my parents were right there to help me get whatever it was I needed.

If there's a young person right now reading this who's had a similar childhood to mine, who wasn't able to work, I would say to you that you shouldn't listen to what anyone else tells you to do. Do what your heart says. If you feel energetic or in your heart that you can do something, there's always something out there for you.

Whether it's an office job, a maintenance job, or DJing at an ice rink, there's always something for everyone out there. In my case, I was very fortunate to have my parents back me up whenever I wanted to do something.

I've noticed that today, a lot of young adults may not want to work hard, or it may seem to be a foreign concept to them. Hard work is important, though, in school as well as in earning money. Marks didn't come easily for me. Because of my mental capacity of that time due to hydrocephalus, I had a lot of problems processing what I was learning in the classroom. I remember sitting up in my room for two and a half hours memorizing facts and figures. My parents used to think I was talking to myself, but what I was really doing was memorizing what I had to learn for a test.

Whatever your situation is, if it's something that you are capable of doing something and you're just lazy about it, then you're not going to be successful. In this day and age, you have to go after what you want. In order to do that, you have to realize the value of hard work, because that's how you become successful. Good things come from hard work.

Hard work may not be what you think it is, either. Hard work can be something as simple as studying for a math test.

Would you rather study for a math test or would you rather be out there playing football?

You have to make that decision. The hard work is often just figuring out what to sacrifice in order to get what you want out of life. I knew that I couldn't play any sports or do anything physical and so my parents always instilled their good values of hard work in me and they would gently remind me that if I worked hard in school, I could realize whatever dream I wanted. That's what they would always say to me.

As always, my parents and my sister gave me guidance that really shaped my life.

My sister was a great role model for me. She worked hard to get where she wanted. To the kids today, let me say this, nothing comes easy. You have to work at whatever goal you have in mind. It's that simple.

The Later Years

My parents always instilled the value of a good education in me. Consequently, education has always been big part of my life since I could not do much else in the way of sports or physical activity as mentioned earlier.

"The difference between school and life? In school, you're taught a lesson and then given a test. In life, you're given a test that teaches you a lesson." (Tom Bodett)

I wanted to always fit in with my friends and when I was in high school, I would at times neglect my studies because I just wanted to make up for lost time from my youth. I will admit that my marks in high school were not the best. I was happy that I had made many friends and that my disabilities were accepted. As time went on however, I realized that if my dreams of becoming a teacher would come to fruition, I would have to work harder.

I've always liked hanging around other kids, and I wanted to do something with children. I didn't want to be a counsellor or child youth worker. I wanted to be with groups of kids. That meant becoming a teacher.

The only problem was that my grades in most classes weren't as good as they should have been.

Hydrocephalus made it hard for me to learn at times. I used to envy kids who could just read something and they had that photographic memory where they could retain information immediately. I didn't have that ability. I used to freeze up during exams. I'd be nervous going into them and given that my brain processing ability wasn't that great, my marks were below what they should have been, certainly not enough to get me into university.

I did the best I could. My parents would say to me that I wasn't studying hard enough, but it really wasn't that. I would be nervous and there were certain subjects that I didn't get. Besides that, I found my retention to be very limited at the time. Also, I didn't understand math and science and I hated history and geography.

But as I would discover in high school, I loved French and English. Those were my strengths, just languages in general.

Back then, when you started high school, you were able to take French as an option. It was something I was really looking forward to. I found that I really enjoyed it and did well. During that time, I realized that I wanted to be a French teacher. That meant I had to be really good at speaking French.

Outside of class, I joined the French club, making new friends who would help me practise.

I really enjoyed learning the language. I would watch my French teacher going through the lessons and I would think to myself, "I could do that!". Every year, I took French and I got better at it. Even today, I'm still fluent in French.

Even though I made a few friends, high school wasn't all about the social time for me. I was still in and out of hospital during the summers. My migraine headaches caused by hydrocephalus were still acting up and making me feel weak and nauseous. At the age of 17 I spend one last summer in the hospital.

When I was in elementary school, in Grades 7 and 8, I found it difficult to communicate with many of my friends. Because of my disability, I had few friends and some of my classmates were cruel at times. I remember being on rotary and I was in the hallway going to my next class when suddenly I had a seizure and fell to the ground. All of the children just walked around me and ignored me. I would even hear mocking words such as, 'What a weirdo!' It wasn't until my friend Leo went to the office and said, 'Roger just fell to the ground. He needs help', that the secretary came out, escorted me back to the office and called my home. Again, my self-esteem took a beating. Back in those days it was very uncommon to see children with disabilities in the same classroom.

Name calling became the norm for me. Throughout elementary school, I became known as 'Chester', a character from the TV western, 'Gunsmoke'. So the odd person would mock me and say, '….coming Mr. Dillon,' which was a line from the show all the while imitating my limp. You can imagine what that did for my self-esteem. Nowadays, that doesn't happen since all children are in the same class with an educational assistant to help them. Children learn from a young age to accept children for who they are and that they are not different.

Furthermore, when I had my second surgery in Grade 6, I returned to school and had to get special permission to stay for lunch. However, at that time, there was no teacher to supervise and therefore I was told, 'you can have your lunch outside, on that rock.' It was November and quite cold. I will never forget how embarrassed I was to endure such a thoughtless act. But that was the rule and we didn't question it. Nowadays students stay for lunch since most parents work and therefore they are accomodated, which I believe is a very good thing for the families.

By the time I reached high school, things seemed to be a bit better, but not until the later years.

I found that kids in high school, especially in Grade 9 and 10 were not very accepting of my disability. Students in those early grades of high school still had the mentality of elementary school children who looked at children with disabilities as being different. I remember in Grade 9 everyone was going to a 'get acquainted' dance and I made a friend whose name was Jack and we went together. While were standing around the music started and I saw this pretty girl so I went to ask her to dance. As I made my way over to her my foot gave out and I fell just as I reached her! When I ask her to dance she abruptly said, 'uh no!' I was mortified! However, once I got into Grade 11 and 12, I started making friends who accepted my disability and who never brought it up, which made me happy. It kind of completed me.

As I said earlier, today, children with disabilities are integrated with their regular class, and I believe that is a great asset. It helps the students realize and accept that everyone is the same, no matter what problem or disability one might have. I wish had that back then.

With having new friends, I had a social life for the first time in school, but I had to work extra hard to make sure to balance my friend time with my studies. Because of my condition, I had to be careful and diligent that I didn't let my learning stop.

If I had to pick, I would say that Grade 12 was my best year in high school. My average was 75%, which was not outstanding but my French mark was always over 90%. As time went on, I realized that I had to work harder and I did. By the time I got to Grade 13, I knew this was it.

Finishing my last year of high school was great, but I was nervous about getting into university with my grades. Back then, the admission bar for university was 60%, and I barely made it, but it was my French mark that put me over the top.

I remember the day I got the letter from McMaster. I received a letter in the mail that informed me that I had been accepted into the first year of Humanities at McMaster University. I was really happy about that!

My brother-in-law Albert, my sister's husband, is worth mentioning here. The year I got accepted into university, I was thrilled, but if it wasn't for Albert, I don't know what would have happened. He guided me through and helped me pick out my courses for first year. He also helped me get through Math in Grade 13, which was a real struggle for me. Albert always encouraged me never to give up on my dream. "You can do this," he would tell me.

Anytime I needed some help, Albert was always there to help guide me.

Unfortunately, he passed away in August, 2017, but he will always have a special place in my heart as always encouraged me to do my best at whatever I attempted to do.

I started at Mac in the fall of 1972. I had reconnected with many of my school friends from Scott Park Secondary and Hamilton Collegiate Institute (Grade 13 school). The only problem was that many of them didn't take French, so I didn't see much of them during the four years I spent at Mac. I even reconnected with friends that I had left behind when I graduated from St. Ann's School on Barton and Sherman Avenue, because they had gone to Cathedral High School, while I went to Scott Park Secondary. It was great to see these people again.

University was different. The teachers wouldn't remind you about homework.

They'd give you a date for a paper or an assignment and tell you that if you didn't' hand it in, you'd get a zero. We were used to being spoon fed for deadlines and that was a big change. I should say that I got off on the wrong foot in the first semester because I had too much fun. I felt that I deserved to have some good times after all those tough years.

By meeting new friends and being a grown- up, I would spend a lot of nights out with them.

Because I was housebound and hospital-bound from the age of 1 to 17, I thought to myself, 'I deserve this.' I decided I needed a little bit of an outlet, such as hanging out with friends. Once I got it out of my system, sometime around the second semester, I really began to focus on realizing my dream goal of being a teacher.

At Mac, I took classes in French and Italian, and got very high marks. One thing I remember was that not a lot of guys took French, so I was always surrounded by girls in my classes. These girls would talk to me like a person and accept me for who I am. That made me feel really good knowing that I could be 'one of the group' and not stand out because of my disability.

Going into second year, I reconnected with more friends that I'd known in elementary school. A few of them, such as my very close friends Tony and Karl, I met in line while in registration. To this day, Karl will still tell the story of how much of a big mouth I was while I was while waiting in line for registration for second year, acting like I knew everything about university and telling all the first year students behind me about all the things you could do at McMaster. Paul and Rick were two other friends that I'm still in touch with today as well.

In third year, I joined the Italian Club at McMaster and we had a play, *'Un Curioso Accidente'* that the club members put on. I wasn't in the play but, Tony, Paul, and I took care of the lighting. I remember one time, we upset the professor so much because we accidentally turned off the lights on stage while the actors were performing. My professor was so angry with us and we laughed so hard it hurt. I could even hear Carla, Tony's girlfriend at the time who is now his lovely wife, laughing from where she was sitting. I had so much fun that year. My friends made me feel so welcome and accepted me for who I was. The friends I made in university have become my life- long friends.

My university years were very notable in that during those years those summers were the first ones that I had all to myself and where I didn't have to go to the hospital. Even though I didn't have any operations, I still had to be very careful about how I walked around, how much I drank and places we went. Having those summers free was like a great weight off of my mind.

Those four years at McMaster went by in the blink of an eye, and before long it was time to apply to Teachers' College. In June of 1976, I graduated Magna Cum Laude with an Honours Bachelor of Arts degree in French and Italian, an achievement that the younger version of myself couldn't have imagined, especially when I was in and out of hospital all the time and most especially when my grades in high school had been so low in most other subjects.

My parents were concerned about me going too far away just in case I would have any kind of relapse, I would be alone and away from medical assistance and doctors who knew my history. More importantly, my family and friends were still here and I wanted to be near them, so I decided to just stay at Mac and go to the Ontario Teacher Education College, starting there in 1976. My focus was on the Primary, Junior and Intermediate Divisions'

Those post secondary years were very important to me, not only for my education, but also personally, as this was the time thatI found my lifelong friends with whom I am still in touch and am very close. My self- esteem in high school was quite low, but thanks to these friends that I made in university and teachers' college, I began to feel accepted as a person again and not as an outcast.

If there's a child reading this right now who is thinking about becoming a teacher, who may be sitting in a hospital bed right now, or sitting at home feeling that it's not possible because of their illness or disability, I want to tell you what my parents told me: you can do anything you want if you put your mind to it.

There are different ways of getting to where you want to be, and you can do it with hard work and staying focused. I believe that hydrocephalus was a roadblock, and if I'd let it stop me, I would never have become who I am today. I knew in my head that I didn't want to be a burden to my family or to society in general. Instead, I wanted to contribute to society.

No matter what illness or sickness you may have, you can always find something suitable for you that is also great for the world. You just have to find your own way. I believe you can.

My Teaching Career

I've shared these stories with you in the hopes that, if you're a young person who's suffering from an illness or a condition, whether it's hydrocephalus or something else, and you're feeling hopeless about what lies ahead for you, that you can find some inspiration in what I went through.

That's why it's important to show you a little bit of how everything turned out afterwards. I'm going to do that by giving you a little glimpse of just what amazing things were waiting for me after I finished Teachers' College.

Once I received my Ontario Teacher's Certificate, I had to set out looking for employment. The first places I looked at, of course, were the Hamilton Catholic and Public School boards. My dream would be to find a teaching job near my family in my own hometown.

However, at the time of my graduation, I found out that the Hamilton school boards weren't hiring. I would constantly call the Board Office in Hamilton to inquire about job openings. There were no new postings. Disappointed, but still committed to living my dream, I looked elsewhere.

In 1976, after having checked around the Hamilton and Toronto areas with little success, I applied for an opening with the Bruce-Grey Roman Catholic Separate School Board, as it was known then. There was a Primary French Teacher position at a school called St. Basil's, way up in Owen Sound, some two hours away from home. Though my parents were a little anxious at the thought of me being that far away, it was the first teaching job I'd managed to get and I wanted to go.

So, with the help of my mom, dad, sister, my brother-in-law Albert, and a few of my friends, I packed up my things and made the long haul up to Owen Sound that summer. I'd found a place to stay and everyone helped me move in. Though it was less than a day's drive, when I saw my family driving away that day, for the first time, I felt alone.

Still, I was in my early twenties now, an adult, someone who had overcome a lifetime's worth of challenges, many of them life-threatening, deep in my heart I knew that this is what I wanted to do for the rest of my life. I was now a proud elementary school teacher about to start living my dream. I could do this.

The fall term went well. I found I was comfortable in a classroom and the students liked me and the way I taught. Before long, I had settled into a good groove and felt confident.

The winter was cold and we experienced the infamous Blizzard of '77' that year, which buried most of southern Ontario in nearly 100 cm of snow, blocking the roads and making it impossible for me to head home to visit or for anyone to come visit me.

It was very hard for me since it was the first time I was away from home and my family. Some people reading this would probably think that I was being childish and immature given my age at the time, but in fact I never really experienced independence since I was always in the hospital or at home. I was always used to having them protect me and knew that I had them near if I needed them. I will admit I was lonely, but I still had the rest of the year in my contract in Owen Sound. Like it or not, I had to get through it.

Winter turned into spring, and before I knew it, it was the last day of school in June. Though I was and am forever grateful for that first teaching experience, I knew that I didn't want to stay so far away from home once again.

One of the advantages of being hired as a teacher was that finding new teaching positions became much easier than when you were a new graduate. This is because you could transfer between different boards and show that you have some experience behind you.

That year, I made the decision to transfer from the Bruce-Grey board and found a position with the Haldimand Board of Education as a French teacher. I said goodbye to Owen Sound and headed south once again, not quite in the city of Hamilton, but within a short drive of everyone I knew and loved.

I would end up teaching French there for ten years in the Junior and Intermediate Divisions. I truly enjoyed my time in Haldimand. In fact, that experience was even more rewarding in that French had never been taught in that area and myself and three other French teachers were hired to pioneer and write the program for the county. The children, staff and schools were a very positive experience for me. To this day, those children, who are now adults, still communicate with me and still respect me as their 'Monsieur.' It's very gratifying to know that I was able to reach these students and make such an impact on them.

Finally, in the fall of 1988, I was able to get a teaching position with the Hamilton- Wentworth Catholic District School Board where I taught French in the Junior-Intermediate divisions. You might say I returned to my roots. I taught for this board for 19 years, the longest time in my career.

For much of that time, my hydrocephalus was stable, still there, but not giving me any trouble. Those times in the hospital felt like they were miles behind me. However, without any warning, I soon began suffering a relapse.

I started experiencing some difficulty walking and severe back pain. I was absent from school for awhile. due to an injury that occurred at school. It was during one of those occasions, more specifically February, 1996 when I was off from school that I slipped on a patch of ice and had to go to the hospital and have my right foot checked out. I was seen by an orthopedic surgeon by the name of Dr. Nikolaj Wolfson.

He examined me and said that my right foot would be fine, but then he noticed the abnormality of my left foot. It was then that he suggested a procedure known as the 'Ilizarov' which is a is a type of external fixation used in orthopedic surgery to lengthen or reshape limb bones as a limb- sparing technique to treat complex and/or open bone fractures.

At this point in my life, did I want to attempt another surgery on my left foot? However, the good doctor convinced me and for years I had good mobility.

Unfortunately, it was short-lived as my back pain returned and I still have issues with my mobility to this day. Still, I am very thankful to him for attempting to better my life a little further.

I have many fond memories of my time with the HWCDSB and have made many friends who are still in my circle today. In June 2007, in consultation with my wife, I made the difficult decision to retire. Although in my heart I could teach forever, I felt it was time to move on as I had completed my years and I felt I wanted to enjoy my life after having given to the teaching profession for 30 years. I believe it was the right decision.

Still, I couldn't stay out of the teaching game completely. When French and Italian language teaching positions opened up at Mohawk College on the Hamilton Mountain, I decided to head back to the classroom, teaching adult students for the first time in my life.

Throughout my career, I've had hundreds, if not thousands, of students pass through my classrooms. Some were wonderful students who mastered the language and went on to bright futures.

Others struggled, as I had struggled, and had either overcome their obstacles or went on to excel in other areas. I've received many thanks from students and parents alike for helping them succeed in the classroom, and in return, I'm just very grateful for the chance to make a difference for them.

To the younger children reading this chapter, you might not find any of this as important or relevant to you right now, and that's okay. You have a lot of time before you'll have to start worrying about jobs and moving towns and careers.

Still, if you have a dream of growing up someday to do something amazing with your life, and you're currently facing illness or disabilities or other barriers, I want you to look over what I just shared with you and find your own version of a future that you can have doing what you love.

Remember the lessons so far that I've shared with you. You'll need to focus, workhard, surround yourself with people who love and support you, and never give up.

Truly, I'm living a dream life, and it only seems fitting to conclude with one last tale, a love story, of how I met the woman of my dreams and of the family we started together.

A Dream Life

During my year at Teachers' College, they had planned a Christmas Formal. I wanted to go, but I didn't have a date.

The previous year, when I was in my last year at McMaster, the campus bar (known as the Downstairs John) was having a Wednesday night pub night. I went with my friends. At one point, we saw a group of girls arriving into the club, one of whom I knew and whose name was Maria.

The band that was playing that night was the 'Downchild Blues Band' who were a very popular group from the 70's. When the song 'Flip, Flop, Fly' came on, I immediately stood up and said to my friends, 'I need to dance this' because it was like a jive/big band type of song to which I loved to dance.

I went over to ask Maria to dance, and she told me "I don't know how to dance to this song, but my cousin does." Suddenly this other girl stepped up, dressed in palazzo pants, a colourful top, and chunky shoes. I took her hand and we had a great time on the dancefloor. We ended up dancing all night long. She truly made a lasting impression on me.

Later, I'd learn that her name was Eveline. I didn't know it at the time, but that night would be the first time I danced with my future wife.

A year later, when I needed a date for the Teachers' College formal, I remembered the fun I'd had with Eveline at that Pub Night and thought to myself, 'I wonder if she will go with me to this dance.' I built up enough courage to call her and said, 'Are you busy Friday night?'

"No, why?" said Eveline.

"The Teachers' College is having a formal and I was wondering if you'd like to go with me."

"Hmm…can you call me back on Friday and I'll let you know?"

I wasn't too happy with that answer.

That Friday night, I remember driving my mother's car and taking her to Eastgate Square. As we entered the mall, I said to my Mom, "I need to use the payphone."

I phoned Eveline back as she requested.

'Oh hi!' she chirped sweetly, apparently oblivious to the very thought that I had been sweating bullets all week long waiting for her response.

"Are you still interested in coming to the formal with me?" I asked.

"Yeah, I'd like to," she said.

All of my friends were there that night. Eveline seemed to get along so well and she felt comfortable with the group that I was with and with all the girls who were there, Joanna, Mena, Sara, Pam and Tina. She knew these girls from Cathedral Girls' High School, so that made it a bit easier. Eveline was a big hit with them as she had everyone on the dancefloor following her moves while she taught them to do 'The Bus Stop', a popular disco dance of the 70's.

Later on in the evening, they all came up to me and said "Roger, she's a keeper!" We had a great night, and as I dropped her off later, I asked her, "do you want to go see a movie sometime?"

"Sure," she said, "how about tomorrow?' I guess I must have made a good impression because no girl had ever asked me out before this. I felt so special!

The next day as per her request, we went to go see "Carrie", the Stephen King horror movie, with Sissy Spacek.

A week later, we went back to see "A Star is Born" with Barbra Streisand.

After that, we started dating, and the rest is history.

We dated all through my time at Teachers' College, and in the fall of 1977, I started with the Bruce-Grey Catholic District School Board up in Owen Sound.

Before I left, I proposed to Eveline who has been a rock for me. She has been very supportive of my limitations and has helped me immensely over the years. It takes someone special to understand and share my trials and tribulations and she was the one to do it. She truly loves me unconditionally.

We were married on August 26, 1978.

Perhaps the happiest day of my life, other than the day I married my wife, was the day I actually had the honour of walking my own daughter, Alicia down the aisle. That was a day I thought I would never see given the circumstances of my health when I was younger. Those were days that were painted as dark and dreary. But as I grew and surrounded myself with people I loved and respected and who loved and respected me in return, that darkness disappeared. The day of Alicia's wedding was another milestone for me. The doctors back then could not tell my parents how much time I would have on this earth. But thankfully, I was able to not only complete my education, get married and have a child, but also to be able to see her grow up, graduate from high school and university and become employed and be extremely successful in her field of Science that she chose and then to top it off, get married herself. For others, it would seem normal. For me this was special.

My message here to children who lose hope is to fight hard, both mentally and physically, against all obstacles. Never give up on your dream and never think there is only one solution. This is what I have learned having dealt with Hydrocephalus.

After leaving the Bruce-Grey Catholic District School Board, I returned to the Hamilton area, and applied to Haldimand Board of Education, which later became the Grand-Erie District School Board, and Eveline and I bought a house together on Hamilton's East Mountain.

During that time, our daughter, Alicia, came into our lives, our pride and joy. That was probably the most exciting time of both our lives. Alicia has also been a very influential part of my life and has taught me that I can do whatever I wish if I am careful and take my time. She continuously encourages me to continue to keep working hard, and not concentrate so much on my past health issues, but rather be steadfast and forge ahead. This has made me a stronger person.

I've learned more patience and perseverance from my daughter than I have from anyone else I know. She is my true inspiration. Alicia has grown up now, gone to school and received her PhD in Chemical Biology at McMaster University and has begun a career in Health Care Research. She married a wonderful man, Peter, who is also in healthcare as a social worker.

Eveline and I are still happily married, and I continue to teach Italian part time at Mohawk College. We still live in Hamilton and have seen the many changes and transformations that the city and the world have gone through over the years.

They say that when you're young, and you have your whole life ahead of you, the future is also wide open. With so much time ahead of you, you never quite know how everything will turn out. But as I sit here in my 60s, looking at the years gone by and the present that I have now, I can truly say that I am living a dream life In life there are roadblocks… and lessons. Hydrocephalus was a major roadblock for me. However, my experiences have also taught me many things. I have learned that one must persevere and keep working hard to concentrate on the good things life has to offer.

Each day I attempt to accept the hand that God has dealt me, and this continues to make me strong. I have also learned to never give up in life. One should not focus on the negative but rather on the positive; some days are better than others, but I am working hard at it.

As I mentioned earlier, I have always managed to live by my motto, penned by the rock group, Trooper:

'We're only here for a good time, not a long time. So have a good time because the sun doesn't shine everyday.' (Trooper, 1977)

I believe we need to seize the day because no one knows what tomorrow will bring.

In spite of my limitations, I have been able to live a full life and with the help and support of friends and family members, my life has been very satisfying and rewarding.

As I said in the beginning, I will say again here at the end. If there is anyone suffering any kind of an illness or setback reading this, my message to you is 'never give up, work to your capacity and do what you can to fulfill your life dreams. After all, we only get to do this once.'

Above all, and as always, I thank God for allowing me forge ahead and to experience all the joys of a normal and happy life.

About the Author

Roger DiBattista is a teacher, educator, mentor, and inspirational author. Diagnosed with hydrocephalus as a young boy, Roger spent most of his childhood receiving medical care, persevering through many difficult and heartbreaking challenges throughout most of his educational career.

Defying the odds and predictions of his doctors all through his life, Roger graduated high school and attended McMaster University in his hometown of Hamilton, Ontario, Canada, where he received an Honours B.A in French and Italian Studies in 1976 and in 1977 his Bachelor of Education and Ontario Teachers' Certificate from Ontario Teacher Education College– Hamilton.

Roger enjoyed a storied career in elementary education for 30 years and has been an inspirational figure to his students over the years, especially those with health and disability-related barriers.

Roger currently teaches French and Italian at Hamilton's Mohawk College of Applied Arts and Technology. Roger resides on the East Mountain in Hamilton, Ontario with his lovely wife, Eveline and is the proud father of a beautiful daughter, Alicia who is married to Peter and they reside in Ottawa, Ontario.

Learn more about Roger by visiting www.rogerdibattista.com.